INVESTING IN RENTAL PROPERTIES:

*A BEGINNER'S GUIDE TO CREATE PASSIVE
INCOME INVESTING IN REAL ESTATE*

Table of Contents

Introduction

Real estate investing is actually much simpler than you realize! It certainly helps to have the right team on your side, especially when you're not exactly sure what you're doing. Basically, having the right team means the difference between failing and succeeding. You'll learn why exactly rentals make the best investments, which property types are best for renting out, and why location matters so much. Your success relies on having tenants, so you need to consider what those tenants are looking for and how to provide it to them. Different properties do well in various types of locations; a multi-family home might not do as well in the city as it would in the suburbs.

Rental property investing is an excellent way to diversify your income. To most investors, this is a great way of boosting their wealth. If you have already decided to invest in rental properties, this is a good move that you have taken. Expect numerous benefits to come your way, including the fact that you will be meeting your financial goals within a specified period of time. Making your decision to become a landlord is not an easy move. The fact that you have taken this bold step implies that you expect the best in future.

To ensure that you invest in a promising rental property, you need to indulge yourself in an extensive analysis of the rental property you are about to invest in. This entails finding out whether you are settling for the best location. Consider factors such as the security of the neighborhood. Talk to landlords within the area to know if the place is secure enough.

It is always wise to bear in mind that being tactful in the real estate business gets you amazing deals without having to spend a lot.

If you have been thinking of investing big, then it is quite likely that the idea of rental property investing must have crossed your mind. Investing in rental properties is what most successful business people do. However, the process of investing your money in rental properties is not as straightforward as you might think. Equally, the process is also not complicated. With a few tips here and there you will land yourself a property that will make you rich.

Rental property investing is a form of investment that has been there for ages now. The houses that most of us live in belong to people. They belong to investors who decided to invest in rental houses to earn something out of it. Deciding to invest in rental properties is not something that you can wake up one morning and decide to do. One of the main reasons as to why most individuals will rush into the idea of investing in rental properties is, of course, the financial freedom benefit that comes with it.

In simple terms investment property is an investment that is primarily purchased to generate income. This type of property is one that is bought for the purposes of either renting it out or reselling it for a profit after undertaking some renovations. There are, however, some variations of this term. One such variation is an instance where a family decides to downsize or relocate to another residence. This property can become an investment property if the family decides not to sell it.

Another example is where one purchases a house that hosts many families. The new owner might decide to live in one of the houses and rent the others. There is also another variation where the owners of the property might decide to be using the property once in a while or during certain seasons as vacation destinations.

You are going to discover everything related to property investing, from the idea of buying your first house to the actual managing of the property. Get comfortable and ready to begin this journey!

Chapter 1: Types of Rental Properties to Invest In

When investing in real estates, you have to know the type of rental properties that you are investing in. The main reason for this is that different properties have got varying ways in which they offer returns on investment. Some are ideal for long term purposes whereas others are preferable if at all you are looking to earn profits within a short period of time. Experienced investors will also argue that knowing the type of rental properties is essential simply because they differ in value. Thus, you ought to determine whether the properties you are going for are within your budget range. This section takes a look at the common rental properties that you will find. With this information, you will end up making sound decisions on the best properties that are worth investing in.

When you are in the market for a new rental property to purchase and fix up, there are actually a few options that you can go with. It often depends on how much you want to invest, how much work you want to do, and how much you would like to make in the process. Each of the rental property types is going to have their benefits and their negatives, but being open to each one and looking at them can make the difference in whether you choose one over the other.

We all know that mistakes happen; accidentally saying the wrong thing, bumping into someone, or dropping what you were just holding. But while these mistakes are pretty small and can be overlooked, choosing the wrong rental property can really mess up your new real estate company. It can mean a lot of unnecessary stress, be very expensive to fix, and even cause you yourself to feel ill. So how do you make sure to choose the best property? There's so many out there, and there's a lot of different questions you can ask yourself to help.

What to buy, what to not buy, how many bedrooms, should the property have a garage, what are the neighbors like, what's the color of the property, how old is it, how big is it. Keeping these fundamental questions in mind will help you to find the best property for your business.

Below are some of the types of rental properties that you can consider investing in.

Single Family Homes

The first option that you can consider is a single-family investment property. This is going to be either a condominium or a house that was purchased by the investor with the intention of renting out to one single tenant (or a family that lives together). Only one tenant or family will live in the property at a time. This has a number of benefits, including only needing to watch after one property at a time, and the fact that many of those who rent these properties are willing to stay in them for some time.

Some of the common ways that you are able to invest in these kinds of properties include buying fixer-uppers, foreclosures, or other types of properties that are undervalued for one reason or another in the area. Your goal is to purchase the undervalued property and then fix it up before renting it out to a single family or tenant. You want to make sure that the actual value of the property is higher, as high as possible, compared to the purchase price.

Single-family homes are the easiest to manage, mainly because those renting them tend to treat these types of houses as if they are their own homes. While some people like living in apartments, most would prefer a house with a yard. However, most people also don't want too big of a house or to buy a house outright, which is why they're renting. It's possible for you to find tenants that would prefer to stay renting a single-family home for decades, which would definitely benefit you. Since the renters see the home as theirs, they also usually do some of the repairs needed and take better care of the yard. And unlike apartments, in single-family homes, the tenant pays all of the utilities, which makes it much easier for you.

Small multifamily investment properties

The next type of property that you can consider investing in is the small multifamily investment property. These are usually going to be either a two unit or a four-unit building. The small multifamily investment is one of the best places for a beginner to start. It allows you to get more than one rental income in a month, which means more profits for you. Even if one of the parts is vacant, you are still able to make an income on the other parts, which can be a lifesaver when you first get started.

There are a few ways that you are able to work with this one. First, you can just have the tenants occupy all of the units. This means that if the property has four units in it, there are four different tenants that are able to pay you each month (unless there is a temporary vacancy). This is the way to make the most significant amount of profit each month, and you should be able to cover the mortgage easily if you can keep the property filled.

Another option is to occupy one of the units. If you have four units, you will live in one of them, and then three other tenants will live in the other units. This can be a great option if you want to keep your debts and your risks down during the time. You are effectively having your tenants pay for the mortgage and your living expenses as well, which can help you get started. Make sure that you are able to charge enough for the rent on the other units to cover you before you decide to do this one.

Large multifamily investment properties

You can also decide to take the step above a bit farther and work with a property that has five or more units. Sometimes, this goes so far as to have hundreds of individual units that you will manage. You will most often see these as apartment complexes. This type of property can sometimes be owner-occupied, even though this is not as common as you will find with some of the other options. But mostly these units are all going to be occupied by the tenants.

The Mixed Use Investment Property

This is another type of investment property that you can choose to work with. It is usually going to be used by the landlord for both commercial and residential purposes, and you are most likely to see this property type in some busy urban areas.

For example, you may have a restaurant in the bottom part, and then a handful of apartments in the top part. It could also be a combination of apartments and offices. The way that it is used will depend on its layout and how the landlord decides to split things up. But the point is that part of it is used by businesses in a commercial manner, and the other part is used as living arrangements for tenants.

While it can make you a good deal of profits, it could limit the number of tenants you have. Many people may not want to deal with the noise of the commercial business being there, and the commercial business may not feel like that is best for them and their customers either.

Retail Investment Property

The next type of property that you may want to consider working with is a retail investment property. This could include one tenant, such as a small ice cream parlor or a larger store like a grocery store. You may also find that things like strip malls that have four or more companies using them can fit into the retail investment property category. Usually, this will include a good deal of space for the tenant but can bring you a nice income if they choose to be there.

There are a few benefits that come with this type of investment. First, you will find that retailers tend to sign longer leases. This allows them to stay in one spot and makes it easier for their customers to find them. This also provides you with a level of stability with the amount of money that you can count on with the property.

However, these are hard to find tenants because most of the tenants are going to be picky. And once one of your tenants move out, it can take a long time before you are able to get anyone else back in and using the property. The success of these retail investment properties will depend on how healthy the economy is as well.

Industrial Investment Property

This is a property type that only one tenant is likely to use at a time. In most instances, it is going to be something like a distribution center, storage garage, manufacturing plant, or a warehouse. It is going to be used for a definite need, and it is likely that once you find a tenant, they are going to be around for a long time.

There are a lot of different types of investment properties that you can choose to work with, and it often depends on the area you want to invest in, the potential that you see in each building, and the amount of work and the amount of profit that you would like to receive from each one.

Since you are a beginner, you wouldn't have the experience, so learning the types of properties in detail is essential. If you have an understanding of the kinds of investments, you would be able to select the ideal investment as per your needs.

Multi-family homes

This is not similar to a single-family property; instead, you would need a particular investment that suits multifamily property. As a beginner, you wouldn't understand the ways to find the right lender. But, with this guide, you can get some understanding of the multifamily home. The whole process will take three weeks or less if you are aware of the process. There are many lenders that offer loans for this kind of property so you can get their help. You can be prequalified quickly with the support of lenders.

The ultimate goal is to find long-term tenants, which is hard to do with single family homes, depending on the family. When there are only one or two bedrooms, tenants might stay for a year or two but eventually move out. Think about it - people usually end up getting married and having kids and need a lot of space for their future plans. By choosing three or four-bedroom houses for your rentals, you're ensuring that your tenants will stay for at least 5 years! And if you ever get to the point of needing to sell, three to four-bedroom houses sell best because, again, of all those families looking for the perfect home.

Vacation rental

Vacation Rental is like the two-in-one benefit because you own a second home that generates income when you are not using it. The best thing about a vacation rental is you will be able to earn profits and offset it to the ownership cost. When you manage your second home with a business touch, you will be able to create a steady income. However, certain factors make rental ownership a lucrative business. Of course, location is essential; meanwhile, there are many more factors that must be considered as well. Your primary goal must be to provide convenience, comfort, and ease to the travelers. In other words, you must make them feel at home. If you do so, it will be easy to find more clients as previous clients will leave positive ratings on the websites where your property is displayed. The effectiveness of word of mouth marketing has not gone out of the market, so you can still hope for it to work for you. So, here are some of the tips you can consider to make your investment worthwhile.

Turnkey

Turnkey investment trading is an exciting type of trading because you would be able to trade from afar. This is the specialty in turnkey investment. You can make passive income in different ways, but this is something out of the box because you gain rentals without actually being there on the property. This means "turn the key." It might sound amazing. But, you shouldn't directly enter the market without learning it. The turnkey market is about the outside local market; you would be exposed to a broader range of opportunities. If you do not know the definition and other details, the turnkey investment may look scary. But, once you learn the details, you can quickly master the investment method. The definition in detail:

The definition is flexible and straightforward because it is "turnkey." A turnkey property is a fully renovated home or apartment building that an investor can purchase and immediately rent out. Turnkey properties are typically purchased from companies that specialize in the restoration of older properties.

Apartment Rental

What about apartment rental? How well are you aware of it? Do you think it is profitable? Well, in the next chapter, we will define the pros and cons of every scenario to define the best way to start. Who doesn't like an additional income? Nowadays, people don't stick to one income source, instead they look for a few sources. So, apartment rental is an option to make additional income.

Of course, collecting a steady income from apartment investment is a great idea. There is a high demand for apartments, that means a higher opportunity to make a steady income. People prefer relocating to a place near their workplace. So, you have to be considerate about the location of the apartment that you are planning to invest in. Also, you need to consider the number of rooms, which dramatically change the price of the purchase and the rent.

Two-bedroom apartments are actually pretty good and liked by a lot of people. People seem to be moving slightly away from suburban life and wanting to live closer to the city. It can be challenging for families because it's hard to find a two or three-bedroom house in a city. So many families compromise and look for a two-bedroom apartment. The type of person can affect your rental business too; you want to rent to a professional, someone you know that will be able to afford your rent. And typically, a single professional person prefers a two-bedroom apartment over a studio or one bedroom. It's extra space for their office or a work out room.

Studios and one-bedroom apartments usually have a high turnover in their tenants, even with a 12-month contract. So, renting out a two-bedroom apartment is a good middle ground for someone looking to rent a place for a few years. You can try investing in and renting out a one bedroom or studio apartments, but you run the risk of a high turnover rate. Of course, it's possible to find a single person that is professional and wants to stay in the apartment long term, but the norm is typically the opposite. If you're looking for the best possible chance to make a profit with an apartment, then a two bedroom makes the most sense.

Chapter 2: Designing a Solid Business Plan

Before investing in anything, you need a solid plan to go with it. The goals that you will create should match with the rental properties that you will be investing in. There are different types of properties that you could invest in, and these will have an impact on how you will realize your financial goals. Choosing the right property to match with your plan is therefore regarded as a fundamental step in the real estate business.

The real estate business plan that you will be formulating should detail the business objectives that you have in mind. In this case, your objectives could be to invest in well-maintained properties that are reasonably priced. Your objectives could also feature the fact that you are targeting qualified tenants who wish to reside in your premises over the long run. The main objective that you will also have to mention is that you wish to generate passive income from your real estate business. These objectives act as a guide on what you expect to gain from your business.

What is your mission statement? The mission statement in your business plan will define the direction that your business will be taking. For instance, your mission could be to provide affordable housing by investing in real estate properties. From this, your mission statement should guide you in settling for affordable houses that will entice your tenants. This is the main goal that you will consider before making any investment decision.

A good plan will also detail the guiding principles that you and your business associates will stick to. Some of the things that you should not forget to include here are the principles that will drive your business to succeed. Think about the tenant selection process. Define this process in your business plan. Make it clear that you will follow a specific strategy when choosing an ideal tenant to live in your premises. Indeed, the right choice of tenant will have a considerable impact on the success of your property investment idea.

It should also be identified that your business partners will always treat the investment as a business. Purchasing real estates costs a lot. You need to have a team that respects the hustle you are trying to make. If you are partnering with your spouse, they should be aware of the fact that you are running a business. Thus, all your efforts should be tailored to making profits from the project.

Your plan should also detail the way in which service should be provided to tenants. This gives your team members a reason to understand that without the tenants, that business would not have been presented. It is from the renters that you get your rental income. Without their presence, the investment would not be lucrative. As such, your associates should be made aware that the customer deserves to be treated with respect at all times. Clearing the air about this matter guarantees that property management is done in accordance with the client's requirements. Most importantly, their maintenance queries will have to be handled in time. This is the best way of keeping the customer happy and motivated.

What will your business be doing to make sure that it succeeds in the market? These are the keys to success. They should also be pointed out within the business plan that you will create. Just like the guiding principles, the keys to success will reveal to your associates about the best direction that they should take for the business to blossom in the market. In real estate business, management is what determines the success or failure of rental property investment. You might have invested a lot of money. But with the wrong management working for you, the investment will not be profitable. It is therefore important that you learn more about the secrets of becoming a good property manager. Some of the essential factors that will transform you into a good property manager will be discussed later in this book.

Another secret to succeeding could be the idea of investing in quality rental properties. Figure out the demands of your target market and approach them with the right product. A real estate agent should help you in settling for quality properties that have got promising cash flows that warrant long term sustainability.

Your business plan should also include the market analysis that you will have to focus on before investing in any rental property. Here, you will have to consider factors such as the industry analysis at large, the specific market size, industry participants, competitors and the market segments. Having the right information about the market will help you make sound decisions about the best property investments that you should choose.

Chapter 3: Factors to consider before investing

There are several factors to consider before making a decision on investing in investment or rental property. Let us look at some of them.

Surrounding

It is not sufficient that you look at the land that you are interested in investing. You need to look at the land that surrounds it or the assets that surround your proposed purchase. If you plan on investing in undeveloped land, then you need to understand what that land has the potential for. That potential is determined and dependent upon what is surrounding it. Many real estate investments include the purchase of land and then the building of an apartment complex on that land. This is a simple example, but it is there to highlight the issue of understanding precisely what you need to do to make sure that your purchase gives you the return you plan on over the time horizon that you are looking at.

Access

Accessing your property is an important aspect of the price in the future and the income that you can derive from over the course of ownership. You must understand the physical access profile of your investment property and the kind of access that you are allowed. You will be surprised by the number of complications that arise because the property one purchase is offset from the main road and requires the permission of the intermediate property owner to get across.

Make sure that you negotiate the access you want to the property you are purchasing before you sign up for the purchase. Once you make the purchase, the negotiating advantage lies with the property owner you need to negotiate with. If you haven't signed up, you can negotiate a contingency agreement, and that would not be as expensive a proposition as if you have already bought the property and are now forced to deal with the consequences.

It is naive to think that just because you purchase a property that you will automatically be given access to it by your neighboring landowners. That is never the case. You have to negotiate this access ahead of time, and the best way this can work for you is if you negotiate the sale price down with the seller for this reason, but, at the same time, negotiate the easement with the neighbor.

Suitable investments are not always just the plain vanilla ones that you see in the classified sections. You can make a hefty return if you are willing to do some extra work, like buying out two pieces of land and giving the landlocked property access.

Future Development

The future development of the area in which you plan in investing is an important consideration. It does not mean that you must only purchase assets that are sitting in the middle of robust development, and it also does not mean that you must purchase assets that have no development slated for the area. The key is to look at a property that is relevant to the plans you have in mind.

If you plan on purchasing the property to build bungalows and the land around your area is looking to build storage units, then you are going to have a bit of a problem. Some bungalow developers purchase the land surrounding the high-end development and either leave it empty or manicure it into a park so as to keep the bungalow property priced well. It creates a bit of a buffer zone.

The best way to get a feel for future development is to do thorough due diligence of the town and county and to hire a real estate lawyer to do the investigation at the county clerk's office about future development in the area.

Environmental Issues

Environmental issues are probably furthest from your mind, but make sure that you change that right now. Any environmental issues that plagued the property before could become your headache after it is purchased. You should check with the EPA or, and with, the state environmental offices if the land or the surrounding area is facing, or will potentially face, environmental concerns.

When it comes to land and property assets, the urgency and critical nature of environmental issues are significant. If you do not do your EPA study and proceed with something that you think is irrelevant, it could come back later and force you to undertake corrective measures that would cost you and alter your returns from what you have projected. That would be the least of your worries if it stopped there, but it may not and may actually compound into penalties and fines due to non-compliance. The environmental due diligence is the owner's responsibility, and ignorance is not a defense, so make sure you get a lawyer that is adept at investigating these matters.

The location factor

Investing in a rental property will give you various options to pursue. You can acquire rental property almost anywhere.

You can have a team of experts manage your property thousands of miles away as an absentee landlord.

However, a large number of landlords prefer having their rental property near them. This is because this option affords certain advantages. It is easier to make sound investment decisions when one is familiar with his surroundings. It also enables one to have excellent purchasing opportunities and comparable values.

Rental property suitability

When investing in a rental property, it is important to consider what type of property you need to have.

Should you invest in a high-rise building or a small single-family house?

The decision will depend on your budget and objectives.

However, for first-time investors, it is advisable to invest in a small way. The reason is simply that it takes some time before one can get a stable income from his investment. During this period, one is also obligated to do loan repayments which, in most cases, come from regular income. It is, therefore, reasonable to invest in a small property which will translate into smaller repayment amount. Should you locate your property in the city or the countryside? Should it be a resort or a residential property? These are issues you have to consider to determine the suitability of your property.

Chapter 4: Why Rental Properties?

Low risk

Rental property investing is a very low risk, which is why it's such a right choice for beginners. You can learn all you need to know about the process of investing in rentals, and either keep up with them or move on to bigger properties. You go through the entire process of buying a rental, looking it over, adding up the various expenses, and learning how to manage it, all without worrying about high risk.

Of course, as a beginner, you'll definitely make mistakes and deal with many issues. But since rental properties tend to have a slightly higher turn around rate, you'll be able to learn from those mistakes and fix them for the future. You'll only make a mistake once, so eventually, you reach that optimal level of success. Plus, doing all the work yourself means you'll be able to understand what goes into managing a property. Which means, at the point when you're financially able to hire someone to manage it for you, you'll still be able to understand what's going on in your property and won't be taken advantage of.

The cash flow

Of course, the number one reason why people consider investing in these rental properties is that it can help them get positive cash flow. Cash flow is going to be the difference in the money that comes in and the money that goes out. This may sound complicated, but it is basically the amount that is yours from the property after you finish paying down all of the other expenses, including your mortgage, taxes, utilities, and anything else that you owe on the property.

As long as you are able to find a property for a good deal, and one that doesn't require a lot of money to fix it up, you will be able to get positive cash flow from your work. You will find that many times the rental prices around the country are historically high, which means that you are likely to make a good profit from your properties, as long as you work with them and set the rent at the right spot.

Tax-free growth

Making monthly payments on a rental property mortgage increases your equity ownership, and that will continue to grow if the housing market stays healthy. The Internal Revenue Service does not count your properties as capital gains until they are sold, meaning your money will continue to accumulate and grow as long as it stays invested in the property. Great rental properties can generate compound tax-deferred growth that can be pocketed in advance by taking out a second mortgage or refinancing your mortgage with a more substantial amount in both of these examples the cash-out deal is tax-free. Also, when you go to sell your home, if you decide you want to buy another investment rental property, you won't be taxed on the sale of the home.

Tax-free cash flow

Taxes only have to be paid on the profit you make from your rental properties; to calculate this amount, add up all of your rental property income and subtract all of your expenses which can include things like mortgage interest, repairs, property taxes, and property management fees. Depreciation is a natural part of owning anything, but that depreciation can be written off a portion of the property's purchase price each year.

Residential real estate is said to have a depreciation timeline of about 27.5 years, so even if you do not spend any money, expenses still accrue-but those expenses can be used to offset taxable income and save money. The higher the tax rate, the more taxes you should be saving. Depreciation can be a benefit in real estate because properties are usually bought with debt.

Savings for retirement

Another benefit is the long-term returns of purchasing rental properties, which makes them a reliable choice for your retirement account. Steady and predictable income coming in every month from your properties with before mentioned tax benefits is a great way to prepare for your retirement financially. Traditional numbers suggest saving about 25x your annual expenses to be able to remain financially independent during retirement. With the usual way to invest including a portfolio of stocks, bonds, and mutual funds, the rule of thumb is to withdraw no more than 4% of your investment portfolio yearly, and that is assuming that the 4% is a combination of interest, compounded dividends potentially the sale of some assets.

The best way to see a consistent return on your investment is to buy properties with little risk and apparent predictability. Purchasing single-family homes in quality neighborhoods, especially those that already have their mortgages paid off reduces your risks and increases your income. Single-family homes tend to attract tenants that stay longer, pay on time, and are mostly self-sufficient, making them great targets for retirement investors. These types of homes that are also located in a good neighborhood are more likely to increase in value with inflation over time, making them even more profitable.

Appreciation

Another benefit of working with rental properties is the idea of appreciation. This is another way that you can earn a good amount of profit as a passive income investor. The growth of value in the asset can really help to increase the bottom line the longer that you hold onto the property. Since many areas are going to see the values of properties go up over the years, the longer that you hold onto the property, the more that it is going to be worth. If you end up selling it later, you can make a nice profit on top of the income you have received from the rental payments.

With that said, this benefit is not something that is going to be guaranteed on every property, so you will need to be careful. While many times we will see that homes tend to appreciate in most areas, you should not just assume that this appreciation is going to happen. In the event that your property does appreciate, it can be a pleasant surprise that you will enjoy the value of your property.

While most rental property investors only plan out long enough that they are going to be renting the property and don't look past that, the appreciation can be critical when it comes to the property. If, after twenty years, you decide that the property is too much to upkeep, or you want to get out of rental properties, the appreciation is going to matter a lot.

Chapter 5: Where Do I Look for Rental Properties?

Now it is time to get into a bit of the fun that comes with rental property investing. We know about the different types of rental properties that you can choose, how to have the right mindset to make all of this work, and even how to find financing. When all of this is ready, it is time to learn how to find the right property.

There are actually a few methods that you can use in order to ensure that you can find the right rental property for your needs. And the more of the methods that you keep open and at your disposal, the easier it is going to be for you to find a property, and find one that is a good deal and will make you money. Some of the ways that you can find rental properties to purchase to start your investment will include:

Networking

To start, look at your network. This is an excellent way for you to get a jump start on finding properties that the general public may not have any idea about. Since these are properties that may not have been listed yet, and the general market doesn't know about yet, it is possible that you can purchase them quickly and get them for a much lower price.

Networking with estate agencies is another effective method of acquiring off-market leads. Set a minimum of three calls a day to different estate agents in your city, asking for properties and stating that you are an investor in search of houses to buy. You will be astonished of how many leads you will find which are totally off-market and ready to be purchased without competition!

Subscribe to networking events and participate at least once a month. This is an elementary and standard method to acquire knowledge and expertise about trends, markets, locations, and is a fantastic way to build a relationship with other investors, which may sell you deals and give you tips to invest.

Find the property online

The next place for you to look is online. There are a lot of different websites that you can look through to find the information that you want. These sites are going to offer you some different resources, including any properties that are simply for sale in general, for foreclosure, and short sale searches. There are even some sites that will offer you property records and information on particular neighborhoods, which can really help you to finish up your analysis on the investment property you choose to go with. In some cases, if you search around, there may be sites in your area where you are able to be at home but bid on live housing auctions.

The first place to look online though is in the MLS or Multiple Listing Service. This is where all the realtors are going to list their properties, and it can at least give you an idea of which properties are for sale. From there, you are able to dig a bit further in order to find the property that is going to be the best for your needs, and that comes in at an affordable price.

Finding the property with a realtor

We talked a bit earlier about how important a realtor could be to your investment. They will be able to walk you through the process, help you to find some of the properties that you may be interested in, answer your questions, and just be there for some help and support along the way. They are great resources to ensure that you are able to get the results that you would like. And since the seller is the one who will pay for them, then it is definitely worth your time to choose to work with them.

Find the property on print media

Print media is another excellent way for you to take a look through some of the local listings. In fact, many people who are trying to sell without an agent, and may be offering their home for a lower price than what you will find in other places, will choose to go with some of these print media sources in your local area. And since a lot of home buyers are not going to take the time in order to find their homes, there is less competition to fight against here.

Take some time to visit auctions

And the final place we are going to explore when you are trying to find a good rental property to purchase is at auctions. If you go to one of these, you must have an idea of the amount that you are willing to spend on the property and then stick with that number. The job of the auctioneer is to get as much as possible for the property, and they will work against you to try and get you to pick a higher price if you keep in the game. Keeping the options out of the game, and knowing the maximum amount that you are willing to pay on a property, will go a long way in helping you to keep your investment safe and can help you to get an actual good deal at an auction.

Chapter 6: How to Finance Your Rental Properties

Traditional lenders

The first place that many investors choose to go when it is time to finance their investment is a traditional bank. These often provide some of the best rates and can be the most secure to work with. But they do require more effort on your part in order to get the loan that you would like. You will usually need to go through a full application process, have a high credit score, good debt to income ratio, and more, to impress the bank, and it can be harder to work with this one and get the financing.

Banks receive a lot of applications for financing on regular homes, car loans, rental investments, and more. They want to make sure that whomever they give a loan out to will be able to pay it back. And so their requirements are going to be much bigger compared to other lending places. But they are able to provide you with the best terms and rates compared to the others, in many instances, which can be a good thing for your bottom line. It is recommended that you at least check these lending places out to see whether or not they can offer you the best deals for what you need.

Credit unions

Credit unions are another option that you can choose to go with. These work similar to banks, but can sometimes offer better rates, and more personalized service because they are local to the area. These are smaller, but they want to see the area they are thriving, unlike a bank, which may care more about the bottom line and not about the people they lend to.

If you are considering working with a credit union, it is important to sit down and talk with them ahead of time, letting one of the loan agents know what your plans are, and going through the requirements with them ahead of time can ensure that you are going to get the right loan product for your needs. The loan officer can then help you to get the application done, will discuss the things that you need to submit, and is going to make sure that you are all set to go.

Individual investors

In some situations, you may be able to work with some individual investors in order to get the loan amount that is needed for these properties. There are sometimes investors in your area who are looking to make some profits on their money, but they don't have the time, or they don't want to do all of the work themselves. They may be willing to pay you to do the work so that they can just earn money in the process

When you do this, you will need to discuss the terms before you get started. Each individual investor is going to have their own list of requirements before they lend out the money, and you need to make sure that you meet up with these. You both will need to sign a contract with each other before the disbursement of the money to ensure you are both satisfied with the terms and ready to get started.

Your savings

Another option to consider is to use your own finances. If you have been able to save up for some time and can find a really good deal on a property, then this could be the option for you. You do need to come up with a decent amount, though, and it doesn't allow you any leverage in the process, which increases the risk in this situation. You have to come up with more money upfront to get started with this, so if it fails, there go your savings.

Paying for the full property out of your own pocket can be appealing, though. You won't be stuck paying off a mortgage for the next 15 to 30 years, depending on your terms, and all of the money can become your profit right from the start. But coming up with that much money can be a challenge without a lot of time.

Even if you don't come up with the full amount, having a decent amount for the down payment can make a big difference. This will ensure that the bank is going to offer you the rest of the funds that you need for the property, and can reduce some of the monthly costs that you have to try to fit into the rent, thanks to the reduction in money borrowed and a lower interest rate.

Asking friends and family

If you have other people who are looking to invest some of their own money and they want someone else to do it for them, then getting those you know in on the deal may sound attractive. This is usually a last ditch effort though. Loaning money between friends and family can often end up with a lot of hurt feelings and problems, and it is best to go with some other options first.

However, if you think that this is the best option, it is one to consider. Before taking any money from those you know, come up with some written agreement that both parties will agree to. This should talk about the amount of money that is being loaned out, the interest rate on it, when it will be paid back, and more. This way, everyone is on the same page, and there are no misunderstandings or hurt feelings in the process.

Selling Some of Your Properties

You could also finance your dream of becoming a landlord by selling some of your stuff. Say you are driving a luxury vehicle. You don't have to drive it if you lack the capital required to finance your investment. Sell it and purchase a cheaper car. This way, you get to set some money aside and finance your rental properties. You could also choose to live in inexpensive residential apartments and save money. There is a lot that you can save in a month if you chose to live in a less costly surrounding. Make a few sacrifices here and there, and you will have saved a lot of money capable of securing a rental property.

Bank Loans

Getting loans from banks is a conventional way of financing property investment. This is one of the main ways in which most people get their funds to make their dreams come true. Getting a mortgage from the bank is a normal thing for most entrepreneurs. Depending on the bank that you will be relying on, the amount of down payment could vary. The down payment expected from you should be a smaller percentage of the actual price of the rental property you are interested in.

Getting a loan from the bank could take days. Banks are always cautious when giving out loans. They want to reduce their risk, and thus, they would want to offer their loans to people they can trust. In this regard, before a bank approves your loan application, they will have to consider factors such as:

Fix-and-Flip Loans

Being a landlord is a great way of increasing your wealth and securing your future. However, investors could also opt to earn money from rental properties without having to hold the properties for a long time. An entrepreneur could choose to get a fix-and-flip loan where they purchase a rental property, renovate it fast, and sell it for profit. This is a quick way of earning money from real estate properties. The benefit that investors accrue here is that they gain their profits in a lump sum. After selling the properties they purchased for profit, they could easily walk away with their profits.

Chapter 7: Having the Right Mindset for Rental Properties

Another thing that we need to discuss here is how to make sure that you have the right kind of mindset before you decide to get into this adventure. Rental properties are not the investment choice that everyone wants to go with. They may sound really great, and they can make you a good amount of profit if you work hard. But not everyone is going to succeed when they decide to start with this.

There are a few essential things that need to be a part of your mindset if you wish to really see success with rental properties. Having these things in place will make it easier to see some of the results that you want and more success in the process. Some of the things that need to be a part of your mindset in order to see the most success have to come from your own personality and mentality.

Let's have a look at the right mindset to have to achieve success, but don't worry if you don't feel close enough to the following, you have plenty of time to exercise and get better!

Create a burning desire for this investment

No matter what you are trying to accomplish in life, or what your goals are with rental properties, in particular, you need to make sure that there is a desire in you to do this, to achieve greatness. Some people are born with the mindset and the talents to do this, but if the desire is strong enough, you can learn how to develop the talents and do well in real estate, even if you are not a natural at working in this industry.

Think about the saying "necessity is the mother of all invention", and this is something that you can apply to the creation of wealth for yourself. If you have a strong enough need or desire, you will do whatever it takes to find a way to make the right changes. So, if you have a strong desire to work in real estate and with rental properties, then you are going to work hard and persevere, even during the hard times, to make your goals a reality.

Get the right network of support

Never think about the idea of getting support as a sign that you have failed, in fact, this is the best way to ensure that you are actually going to see the success that you want. When it comes to almost any endeavor that is worth having, especially in rental properties, you will need to have other people around to help and support you. At a minimum, consider having a mentor, a network of those to help with properties, and a real estate agent to help.

Develop a plan

Before you ever start to look at properties or into funding for the rental property that you want to purchase, sit down and come up with a plan. This plan will ensure that you are able to stay on track and will keep you out of trouble. All investors who just jump right into the process of rental properties without a plan will end up failing. They will get distracted, forget things, and just generally have a tough time making things work.

The more details that you are able to add into your plan, the better off you will be. Consider a plan or the way that you will get your financing, plan out the requirements that you will want in a chosen property, how much you will pay, and all of the steps that you will do until you grow your empire. There are no limits here, but writing out the steps, the expectations, and what you are going to do will ensure that you are able to stay on track and see the results that you plan on.

Be willing to take risks

To get into real estate of any kind, you have to be willing to take some risks. There is a chance that you will get into this and not make any money. There is a chance that you will purchase a property that is going to cost too much or that will have too much work on it and you spend too much. There is a chance that you will have trouble finding suitable tenants to live there.

When it comes to working with rental properties, there are a lot of things that can go wrong. While you always hope for the best, there are times when things aren't going to head in the direction that you want. You have to be able and willing to take on these risks and do anything possible to prevent these risks before you even jump into the market.

Able to get up and take action

If you like to wait around to take action, or you like to let others take action for you, then rental properties are not the right choice for you. While you should have a team of individuals who can help you out, for the most part, these investments are going to require you to work for yourself. There won't be someone breathing down your neck to get the work done. If things fail, and you weren't doing the work, then it is all on you.

Having the right mindset when it comes to investing in rental properties can make all of the difference. It ensures that you are able to see the results, and put in the hard work, all at the same time. While rental properties can make you a lot of money, they are not the right investment tool for everyone. Having the right mindset and being prepared for hard work, as well as the profits, can make a difference.

Chapter 8: How Much Money Does One Need to Invest in Rental Properties?

Now, how much does one need to invest in rental properties? Unfortunately, it is quite sad that most people would give up on their dreams of investing in rental properties simply because they thought that it was too expensive for them. Other potential investors end up thinking that real estate investment is beyond their reach. It is due to these reasons that most people give up without ever trying to invest in what could have been a game changer for them.

An interesting thing worth noting is that few people know that they could invest in rental properties without raising 100% of the required money. Certainly, if you were aware of this, then, it wouldn't have been a problem for you getting the right funds to initiate your investment. When one looks at the math of investing in real estate, they end up losing hope knowing very well that their monthly incomes cannot sustain the investment idea that they are about to take up. For instance, assuming that a lucrative rental property goes for $200,000. With this price, it would be impossible to invest in the property if one began saving $200 monthly. It would take around 83 years to get the entire amount. So, if you have this mentality, then it is impossible for you to look past the financial limitation that might affect you.

With regards to the issue of financing your real estate investment plan, you need not have the entire cash. In fact, most investors use leverage to purchase their rental properties. What does leverage mean? Simply stated, leverage refers to the process whereby you use some borrowed capital as a way of funding your investment. The advantage gained here is that without raising 100% of the money required, you can settle for a larger rental property. For your investment, it means that you would have increased your chances of getting higher returns on your investment. In other words, you will be making more money by using other people's money.

How Leverage Works

The first thing that you could do with your money is that you are at liberty to purchase a $50,000 rental property since you have the cash. With this option, there is no leverage that is produced.

Secondly, you also have the freedom of going for a bigger rental property worth $100,000. Settling for this option will require you to go for financing options such as a mortgage loan. The loan will only cover the amount of money that you don't have, i.e. $50,000. The amount of leverage that this option will produce, therefore, is 50%.

That's not the end of your options. You could also choose to go for a better investment deal where you settle for two rental properties worth $100,000 each. Here, it means that you will be investing in assets worth $200,000. The amount of money that you have is $50,000. So, the leverage will cover $150,000. This equates to 75% leverage. Do you see the advantage that you will be getting here? You will have spread your risks and invested in two properties, perhaps in different areas.

Now, after some time, your property will gain appreciate by some margin depending on how the market fluctuates. Let's consider a situation whereby the market value of your assets appreciated by 6%. In this case, the first investment option will only gain you $3,000. This implies that your property value would be $53,000. In contrast, the second option will gain you $6,000, meaning that your property value would be $106,000. For the third option, your property value would be twice what you have in the second option; hence $12,000.

Keeping the leverage math in mind, it means that leverage gives an investor the advantage of gaining more from an asset without having 100% of the required capital. Consequently, before spending your entire savings on a rental property that appears lucrative, you ought to think about leverage.

Ideal Conditions for Leverage

Leverage sounds like the perfect plan for investing in real estates. Well, it is. With a smaller amount of the capital that is required, you can increase your chances of getting better returns on investment. Nevertheless, we all know how the economy fluctuates at times. Therefore, it is worth bearing in mind that there are certain ideal conditions for you to use leverage. When these conditions prevail, you can proceed to use leverage to finance your investment ideas.

The best time to use leverage to finance your rental properties is when the values of these assets are increasing. When the values of your rental properties are increasing, it means that in ten years time, your property will have a higher value as compared to today. Obviously, this would be regarded as a good investment. Conversely, if the values decline or stagnate, you should think twice before relying on leverage. The option would not be advantageous since loan repayments will be cancelling out the profits that you should be getting. In the event that this happens, you will be feeling as though the rental properties are a burden instead of an investment.

Luckily, in most countries, properties appreciate in value. This is influenced by the fact that there is an ever-increasing demand for houses. Remember, the population is also continuously rising. Thus, given a period of time, there is a certainty that there would be an increased demand for houses. Hence, rental assets will definitely increase in value.

Using Leverage Cautiously

Getting confused along the way as you plan to invest in real estates is something that happens to every investor. Nevertheless, with a few pointers to light your way, you will be cautious enough to make the right decisions. The following are pointers that should help you in making good use of leverage.

Set Lower Expectations

After researching about the environment that you wish to invest in, you might have found out that rents increase at an average of 4% yearly. With this information in mind, you should not raise your expectations too high expecting that the same will happen in years to come. This might not be the case. You should bear in mind that there are other external factors that might change this over the coming years. So, it is wise to lower your expectations as this ensures that you are not disappointed if things don't turn out as expected.

Stick to a Flexible Payment Plan

At first, paying your leverage interest might not be a challenge. However, think about the months and years that you will be paying. Consider the fact that anything can happen to your finances. You need to settle for a payment plan that you can live with. Don't stress yourself financially as this is something that you might not be fit to handle, more so in these harsh economic times.

Cash Flow is Important

The on-going cash flow of your rental property is one thing that you should not overlook. You should strive to find a way whereby your rentals are occupied continuously. This will make sure that your cash flow is maintained. Keep in mind that you are investing to make profits. Therefore, don't just assume the empty rooms that people will not be occupying. If there are damages that need to be attended to, ensure that you deal with them as soon as possible.

With these tips, you should make use of leverage wisely since you will not feel financially stretched out. Moreover, you will be comfortable knowing that your tenants are helping you sort out a part of the loan that you acquired.

From the information on leverage, it is evident that there is no clear answer as to how much you need to invest in rental properties. There is a wide array of financial options that are at your disposal. All you need to do is to find a plan that works for you. Remember, it is imperative to make sound financial decisions that will not haunt you in the near future.

Chapter 9: Landlord Considerations

Deciding What to Charge

When you are ready to determine what you are going to charge for your rental, the first thing you will want to consider is what is the current average rental price for similar properties in your area.

From there you will want to take what you paid for the property into account, especially if you are going to be making payments on the property as you will ideally be able to have the renter cover the price of the mortgage while still making a monthly profit after paying the property management company as well.

With that in mind, it is essential also to understand that every single rental is different which means that if you feel there is something special about your property that really sets it apart, then you should ensure that the price reflects that as well.

Additionally, it is important to keep in mind that you never want to sell yourself short, as if you do, you are going to be stuck with an undervalued rental until the current tenant moves out.

Choosing the Right Tenants

Once you have been able to secure your first real estate property, now all you need to do is choose the right tenants that won't turn your dream of financial investment into a nightmare. You are actually very close to begin the process of getting a return on your real estate investment. What is important now is that you choose your tenants wisely.

Simply, be firm in your tenant screening process, and you will be reaping the rewards of profiting from your real estate investment sooner than you might think.

The primary profit problems many landlords run into is not thoroughly screening their tenants. Therefore, you must make tenant screening a priority when deciding to rent out your real estate property. Your investment can only be profitable when your tenants pay their rent on time and do not damage your property. Even if you require a security deposit to cover any damages, the overhead and time it takes to manage the repairs at your property will eat away at your income.

It is important to state that there are options to check out future tenant's bill-paying habits by merely running a credit report. Also, you can see if a prospective tenant has a criminal history by running a criminal background check and contacting their former landlords.

You can actually do quality background and credit checks for as low as $15. This investment is worth it to avoid losses from possible dangerous activity or non-paying tenants.

The Lease

Once you have found a tenant that meets your qualifications, the next step is to create a lease that you can both live with which also clearly protects your rights as a landlord while also taking the tenants' rights into consideration as well.

In order to create a lease where both you the landlord and the tenant will agree to, it is crucial to make sure to write down all the details that are important to you regarding renting out your property. At the same time, don't overdo it but make sure that the lease lets the future tenant know what you expect from him/her when renting out your property. When in doubt, put all critical information in the contract to avoid any future problems when renting out your property.

By making sure everything is nice and clear upfront when renting out your property to a future tenant, you will feel more comfortable renting out your property because you are making the prospective tenant aware of your expectations when it comes to renting out your property. At the same time, the future tenant will have a clear understanding of your expectations and will more likely respect the lease and the rental property as a result of you being open and direct about your expectations.

In addition to the things that are and are not allowed in the lease, it is recommended to have a very clear list of consequences for what will occur when things that are not allowed to take place.

Chapter 10: How to Buy a Rental Property

If after considering all the pros and cons you have decided to purchase a rental property, congratulations! The next step is scoping out the right property for you. A good rule of thumb is to start locally when purchasing a rental property. Don't worry so much as to purchasing local so you can act like a hawk over the property and constantly check on it. The crucial aspect is to buy a quality home, not necessarily a home that is close to you.

Conduct your research

Research market conditions in your area, desirable neighborhoods, and what a fair market price is for homes that could be excellent rental properties. Ask yourself, 'why should I get this home'? Starting in an area or neighborhood that you are familiar with is a good strategy for your first property. If you don't want to buy locally in an area you know personally, drive around the zip codes where you want to potentially purchase in and talk to neighbors and shop owners about their thoughts on the area. See if you can find out local development plans too- this will tell you if people and business are planning on moving into town or out of town to give you a better feel for the current and future market potential of the proposed home. The type of home you purchase, where the house is located, and what the neighborhood makeup is can significantly affect who your renters will be and what they value.

Homes in nicer neighborhoods will cost more to purchase up front but will have a bigger payoff for you down the road because the houses can be rented out at higher rates; homes in less desirable or dilapidated neighborhoods show lower income earnings and either an inability to make improvements or the homeowner does not care enough about the property to make it look nice. These neighborhoods will have a higher tenant turnover and probably less desirable tenants applying to live on your property.

If you decide you don't want to stay local necessarily, consider purchasing all your properties in at least the same state. There are so many inefficiencies in having properties spanning several countries due to different laws regarding taxes, having to have more than one property manager, and farther trips for checking in on your rentals. Don't try to spread yourself too thin. Bundle your properties into one, maybe two markets in order to be efficient, save time, and save money.

Pay attention to the condition of the house

You don't want to spend too much money on upgrading a property, especially your first one when you aren't sure yet if owning rentals are right for you, or if your plan hits a snag. For your first home, we highly suggest you hire a qualified professional to inspect the house and get quotes from contractors for any major jobs that would need to be completed.

Look to purchase a house that has good bones meaning it has quality construction, a robust infrastructure, functional floor plan, spacious rooms, and character and natural light. When deciding if a house is right to purchase as your rental property, check for the following:

Quality of home construction

Do the floorboards bounce and creak as you walk through the house? Look at the doorways, joists, foundation wall, front porch if there is one and note the condition of the roofing as well. A good bet for quality materials includes stone and brick on the outside of the home and hardwood floors on the inside.

A solid infrastructure

It's relatively easy to replace plumbing and aging shingles, but if a quality foundation, heating, and electrical systems to name a few are already in good shape, potential renovations will become much more manageable. A solid roof and foundation are also important as they are some of the most expensive elements to fix or replace in a home.

Conducive floor plan

Do you feel a good flow between frequently used rooms, and are the rooms placed in the most common sense way? Note the flow of traffic and whether the current set up is find the way it is or if you would need to do some renovations to fix that. Moving or taking out walls in a home can turn into a significant project, so make sure you know what you are getting into with a property if you are willing to overlook the floor plan. The flow between rooms throughout a house can make or break interest in a home from a renting standpoint: it should be easy to get from one room to another, and related rooms should all be near each other.

Spacious rooms

Are the rooms in the home a useful size and shape? Are there enough rooms for the ideal family you would want to rent the house? Any older homes were much smaller than modern homes built to accommodate growing family sizes. Again, note your thoughts on the rooms, and if you would need to make any adjustments to make the rooms more appealing or functional.

Chapter 11: Keys to Rental Property Success

Rental property investing is a good business only if you know what you are getting into. It is not surprising to find someone failing in this kind of investment, and yet they have a lot of money. At times, it is the ideal manager in property investment that emerges victorious. To guarantee that you make the right moves in your investment, you need to dig in deeper into the world of real estates. You need to learn more about how the market operates. If there are challenges that would be faced in future, you ought to be aware of them. Equally, rental property investing implies that you will be dealing with the bank most of the time. Consequently, it is up to you to make sure that you partner with the right financial institutions that will not disappoint you when you need their help.

Investing in rental properties is a bold move. Without a doubt, it is one of the surest ways of boosting your wealth in these economic times. Nonetheless, perhaps it must have crossed your mind that you need to find out what successful investors do. Learning from the best saved you from the risk of losing your money or merely incurring losses from the investment activity.

Effective Management

One exciting thing about residential property investing is that you will amass enormous wealth if you play your cards right. Nevertheless, to be successful, you also need to learn how to become an effective and efficient manager. As a wise manager, there are times when things will not flow smoothly. During these moments, you need to stand up and make sure that you deal with the situation. These are the times when your tenants might not be paying rent on time or simply failing to follow your rules and regulations of living in your premises.

A good manager should be in a position to balance their finances appropriately. Getting your rental income and committing funds to a different place might not be a great idea. You should be aware of the fact that repairs might come up anytime soon. So, part of your shrewdness should be evident in how you manage your finances. Owning rental properties does not necessarily mean that you are already rich. Since you need a steady source of income, you should pay attention to the mundane activities around your rental properties.

Always Avoid Hot Markets

Hot markets will undeniably be part of your initial target in rental property investing. Markets that appear lucrative are always enticing. Nonetheless, you need to consider everything before rushing for a deal that sounds profitable. Remember, investing in rental properties is something that you can choose to do it in the long-term. Don't be anxious about the fact that you can make millions overnight. Give yourself time to grow in the business. Doing this helps you a lot in avoiding any unforeseen risks in the markets you will be choosing.

So, why avoid hot markets? Hot markets are just risky. You end up risking your investment in assets that you anticipate they will keep rising. What if the market stagnates immediately after you purchased the properties? What happens when the unexpected occurs? Obviously, you are at higher risk if you opt for hot markets. Therefore, you should research on markets that are profitable and yet they are not regarded as hot markets. Leave these markets for experienced investors that are willing to risk everything with the hopes of making their dreams come true overnight.

Don't Invest Too High or Too Low

Making the right choice of your investment property would have an impact on the success of your business. There are landlords that would be tempted to invest highly in rental properties that are promising. One thing that they should realize is that there is a considerable risk that is also associated with such investments. Investing too high means that your margins will be too thin. You could run the risk of reducing your profits by investing too much.

Equally, investing too low has got its risks. Chances are that you could face countless battles with tenants that are disturbing. Rough neighborhoods might be cheap but have you thought about the expenses you could incur just to give the premises a facial uplift. The location of the rentals could also discourage people from living in the area. This could have an impact on the occupancy rate of your houses. Therefore, investing too low or too high is not advisable.

If you are not sure about how to find the best deals in the market, you can always seek the help of professionals. There are numerous realtors in your local market that would be willing to help at a fraction of the cost. So, it is wise to rely on them as they would warrant that you make the right decision from the word go. Know the Costs Up Front

Understand the Market

I tend to think that this key strategy to becoming a successful investor should have topped the list. Indeed, a rule of thumb in rental property investing is that you need to understand the market. You need to find out how much a house would go for in the market that you plan to invest in. Your research of the market should also entail finding out what appeals to people within the area. For example, if you are buying rental property in an area close to university students, you need to know exactly what appeals to them.

If the market is a family-friendly neighborhood, you also need to know what these people are after. Are they after a three or four bedroomed houses? These are some of the factors that most tenants consider before renting a home. Think about whether the residents are most concerned about security. If yes, then your rentals should also have tight security to entice people within the environment.

Getting to know how the market has been doing will also place you in a better position to invest in a market that has seen stellar development. In this case, your aim would be to avoid markets that have stagnated for years. Invest in an area where you see potential growth in the next 5 to 10 years.

Increase Income

Another winning tip in rental property investment is that of increasing income gained from your residential properties. This does not imply that you go out increasing rent for your tenants. No! The idea is that your rental property value should always be on the rise. This implies that your residents should rent your assets at the market price and not anything lower. This assures you that you are getting value from your investment. Well, you might choose to lower your rental rates, but make sure that you do not go way beyond the market price. Keep your prices steady and watch how the market is moving.

Decrease Expenses

Running a profitable business is an investors dream. Well, an issue arises when it comes to expenses. If you don't cut down your costs, you can rest assured that this will affect your proceeds. In rental properties, you ought to aim to reduce your expenses to zero. However, it doesn't mean that you should ignore complaints from your tenants that they need their repairs done.

A trick to reducing your overall expenses is by transferring them to your residents. For instance, electricity bill, water bill or garbage bill. You could transfer them to your tenants. If your premises are worth living, they won't find this as an issue. Also, work to save on electricity by making use of efficient appliances. The same case applies to your insurance coverage. Research on the best companies that offer lower prices for coverage. Minimizing expenses here and there will undeniably help you cut on your expenses.

Seek Professional Help

Quite likely, investing in rental properties is not the only thing that you are doing. Maybe you have a career to attend to. This means that you don't need to sacrifice your career for the sake of managing your rental properties. You could always hire a professional for the job. A rental property manager will help in making your life easier. This works best when you have a number of properties that need to be managed.

Professional assistance will not only come from a manager. There are other experts that you will need to help you out. For instance, you will often need the help of an accountant, electricians, plumbers etc. These individuals are experienced in their respective fields. Cutting on your expenses should not push you to try and repair your properties on your own. You might end up wasting time and doing shoddy work. What you need to do is to seek professional assistance whenever you need it. Time is money. So, if you wish to save your money, cut the chase and ask an expert you help you out.

Understand Your Tax Laws

Knowing your tax regulations will also help you a big deal. Being a landlord implies that you will be eligible for tax reductions. Nevertheless, this is something that you will not be told about often. Accordingly, you need to stay up to date with tax laws within your state. This guarantees that you will know the right times to file for tax deductions. Ideally, this is a move that will also cut your expenses and warrant that you run a profitable business.

Manage Your Feelings

Surprisingly, there are those investors that will fall in love with rental properties that they would be investing in. Well, this is a huge mistake that you should never fall for. Falling in love with the assets blinds you from realizing whether the deal is too good or not. One thing that you should have at the back of your mind is that the properties are meant for your tenants. Other people will be living on the premises. Hence, keep your feelings to yourself. Bringing your feelings to the real estate business will give you the assumption that you might lose out on a deal that was lucrative. Understand that there are numerous rental properties ups for grabs in different locations. You only need to do thorough research for the best deal in the market.

Focus on Long Term Tenants

Have you ever wondered why there are investors that only seek for single-family homes? Well, what these investors are doing is that they are saving themselves from the burden of short term tenants. When your tenants leave your premises, you will lose both the tenants and that you will incur costs in patching up your rooms. Most people will not enter a house that is not repainted after another tenant leaves. Accordingly, you should take the necessary steps to convince your tenants to sign long term leases. In the long run, you will realize that you would have saved yourself a lot of money.

Successful rental property investing also demands that your rentals should always be in good condition. Tenants will always bug you with issues. There will be leaks, falling roofs, broken toilets etc. These are minor maintenance demands that you need to attend to. They not only guarantee that your assets are in excellent condition, but it also saves you from constant laments from your residents.

Keep Your Tenants Happy

Nothing beats the comfort of living in a house where the landlord always listens to you. Put yourself in the shoes of a tenant. They always want their demands fulfilled. The last thing they need is an ignorant landlord that never repairs their premises. If your tenants have been pushing you with an issue, talk to your manager about it. Make sure that everything is done on time. If there are any installations that should be done, do it before your residents get tired. Happy tenants will give you peace of mind. You will never worry about your assets as it would mean your residents are not facing any issues living in your properties. So, as you strive to be successful in investing in rental properties, don't forget the fact that the customer is always right.

Chapter 12: Creating Your Dream Team

When you are ready to get started with your new investment, you need to make sure that you have the right people around you all of the time. It is so important to find a few good people who are willing to help you out, the ones who can answer your questions, get the work done, help you find properties, and so much more.

Finding a realtor

The number one thing that you should consider when you are getting into rental property investing and to help you lower your risk is to find a real estate agent. Many beginners assume that they do not need one of these professionals. They think that they will do better on their own and that it won't be that hard to find a property and get it all closed on. They may even worry that hiring a real estate agent is going to cost them more money, and since they are trying to keep their costs down to a minimum, they decide not to use these.

Working with a lawyer

A real estate lawyer will be able to help you with this. They have the right paperwork, and the proper knowledge, to make sure that you are protected during the whole home buying experience. They can hand you copies of the paperwork that you can sign and then use with the seller. Or, if the seller ends up submitting some negotiations or other paperwork to you, you can take this information to your lawyer and have them look it over.

Finding a good contractor

If you are able to get a property for a reasonable price, it is likely that you will still need to fix it up, at least a little bit. You will be amazed at the things potential home buyers will turn their nose at, and often it only takes a few dollars from you and a bit of time and effort to fix that issue and get the property looking better.

When it comes to these little fixes, you will be able to do the work on your own. It is just fine to save some money and pain with all of the bedrooms or the whole house by yourself, rather than paying someone to do it for you. But there are going to be times when there needs to be more work done on the property, and this will end up going past your level of expertise. When this happens, it is time to call in a contractor to help you out.

The value of a mentor

Another person you should consider adding to your team while we are at it is a good mentor. A good mentor can really help you to take the right steps to see some success with this whole endeavor. They can answer your questions, help you when things get stuck, give advice, and so much more. A good mentor, if you can find one, can prove to be a valuable asset.

As a newbie in the world of real estates, there are a lot of things for you to digest in a single day or month. What's more, even the most experienced investors need help. They need financial assistance to understand whether they are making the right decision or not. And after all, we all need a push sometimes. When things get rocky, you need someone that will keep motivating you to continue investing in a particular business.

Having said that, you need a mentor on board. But the question that you probably are asking yourself is, why do you need a mentor. First, an ideal mentor will advise you on the best properties that you should go for depending on your financial strength. Indeed, there are instances where you might be tempted to go for expensive rental properties since you can seek financial help. Your real estate mentor will prevent you from making mistakes along the way. The best part is that your mentor will also guide you through the best ways in which you can protect your cash flow. If there are external investment decisions that you need to make, your mentor will be there to help you out.

Make good use of the time that you spend with your mentor. You want to make sure that you are asking the right questions and getting as much advice from the mentor as possible, without wasting your own time or their time. Keep in mind that these individuals have already gone through a lot of the uncertainty, the risk, and the same situations that you have, they have a wealth of knowledge to help you succeed.

Accountant

You'll want to make sure your business is set up legally, and that's something an accountant can help with. You also don't want to have to worry about taxes and everything that goes into it. Not only can taxes be confusing for a business, but if you mess up, then you might get audited by the IRS and possible owe a lot of money.

Attorney

Another person you absolutely need to have on your team is an attorney. They can help with all the necessary paperwork and contracts, which you'll be writing a lot. You'll need agreements between you and the tenants, between you and your loan people, and between you and anyone else you end up working with. One small mistake in a contract can mean you end up losing money and possibly even your property. Contracts are also critical if you end up being taken to court

Property Inspector

You need to know the condition of the home you're interested in investing in, whether it's a good deal or just not worth it. A good property inspector can help you to understand everything that's needed to make the potential home worth renting out. The property could look perfectly fine, but an inspector does more than just look at the cosmetic value. They look into the wiring, plumbing, the roof condition, the condition of the insulation, and even the structural integrity. They look over everything and helps you to know exactly how much of an investment you'd need to make. Having one on your team is definitely a benefit to you and to them. You can keep using the same inspector for each property, especially if you know they're very thorough and take their job seriously.

Mortgage Lender

You really want a great mortgage lender on your team. Someone who asks you questions knows their industry and provides you with several options to meet your specific needs. It's up to you to be responsible for each document you're signing and having a mortgage lender who actually takes the time to explain them to you will definitely benefit you. They can help you with any issues that come up and work with you if anything happens to your current mortgage program. You need one who stays in touch and makes sure that you close on your loan in a timely manner. It's entirely possible to end up losing a lot of money because of a bad mortgage lender, so make sure you find one that is really good.

Real Estate Agent

Besides having a mentor in your real estate investment team, you also need a real estate agent. Don't allow the online research that you made convince you that you don't need one. Certainly, you need an experienced individual in real estates to help you maneuver your way to success. The main reason why you should think about working with a real estate agent is that they will help you save time. It's true! When working with an agent, you don't need to know everything. As long as you trust that you are hiring the right person for the job, you can safely invest in rental properties.

Before hiring any realtor, you should consider the benefits that you would gain in relying on one. So, what are some of the benefits that you gain by seeking help from a realtor?

A real estate agent also comes handy due to the very fact that they don't have their feelings attached to the investment you are about to make. This implies that they are capable of negotiating for a better deal than you. They have the confidence of walking away from a deal that sounded too good to be true. Ultimately, they will settle for a good offer that you will not regret putting your money into. Consequently, don't focus on the amount of money that you will be paying your realtor. Instead, think about the convenience that they would be offering you.

Bookkeeper

Managing your finances is an essential part of your real estate business. Often, you will need reports on how your business is performing. This can be done on a monthly basis if at all, you have several rental properties to the manager. Those that have a few units could do this after every three months. You might fail to have the desired financial skills to do business management tasks. Therefore, this calls for the help of a bookkeeper.

How will a bookkeeper help you in your business? There are a wide array of things that a bookkeeper can help you with. For instance, they would help you in issuing invoices to your tenants. This is an activity that would have to be done on a monthly basis. If there are any repairs that have been done on your premises, a bookkeeper will receive invoices from the contractors you will be working with. Likewise, a bookkeeper would also record any cash payments that have been made to your business operation. At the same time, recording bank deposits will also be part of their job.

Insurance Agent

Your rental properties need to be insured against specific unforeseen issues. The main reason why you need to cover your assets is that they cost a lot of money. In the event that there is a fire within the neighborhood, and it ends up catching your properties, you need to be assured that you can recover your property. The same case applies to your rental income. When a fire destroys your rental properties, tenants will have to look for alternatives. This implies that no one will be paying rent when your houses will be unlivable. Thus, you need coverage to guarantee that you can still earn something when the unexpected happens.

Working with an insurance agent warrants that you know of the key areas where you need coverage. Without the right knowledge, you might be tempted to settle for covers that are not reliable. Nevertheless, a skilled insurance agent will not forget to point out the nitty-gritty aspects of covering your properties. For example, they should remind you of the fact that you need to ensure your properties before renting them out. The insurance company should be informed way before you bring in people to rent your homes.

Chapter 13: Analyzing a Rental Property

After making up your mind that you will be investing in rental properties, the first thing that you will be doing is to head out to the market to find the right properties to invest in. There are numerous rental properties up for grabs. However, you need to determine whether this is the right property that you should invest in. Your aim should be to evaluate whether the property will generate the profits that you anticipated. To be certain that you are making the right investment decision, you need to analyze the rental properties. The process of analyzing a rental property entails determining whether the assets are viable both for renting out as well as for profit purposes. During your analysis, you have to keep in mind that your goal is getting something from your investment. This is a business. Consequently, you need to invest in rental assets that will earn you some proceeds.

There are a number of factors that you will have to mull over while analyzing rental properties. Some of these factors will have a considerable influence on how your properties will be performing in the market. Other factors will help you in determining the number of returns to be expected from your investment. This is part of your analysis process. This section will guide you through some essential factors that you ought to consider.

Location

In the world of real estates, location means everything. The location of your rental properties will dictate the way in which tenants will be responding to it. Therefore, it will also influence your marketing strategies in ensuring that most people are aware of its existence in the market. Investing in properties that are in proximity to a university will demand that you target students or the faculty population. Hence, your marketing strategies will focus primarily on these audiences.

Comparable Properties

After pointing out an ideal location worth investing in, the next thing would be to look around for comparable rentals. Take a walk and evaluate how similar houses within the same vicinity pay their rents. Your goal is to know how much people are paying for their rents and other amenities. Important factors to consider when making comparisons include the closeness to each other, size of the rentals, number of bedrooms, condition, and amenities.

Rental Strategy

Part of your analysis will be to evaluate whether your properties will be best rented on a short or long-term basis. The rental strategy that you adopt will have an impact on your rental income. Knowing the best approach to go for guarantees that you settle for an option that is more profitable. You should note that the rental strategies will vary depending on the market you would be dealing with. Undeniably, there are tenants that would not want to lease your property on a long-term basis. Thus, you should make a thorough analysis of the rental strategy that works for the premises on sale.

Type of Property

Which type of properties do you wish to invest in? There are many forms of properties in real estate business; some include single-family homes, townhouses, condos, and luxury homes. Your analysis should be to determine the best properties that suit your financial goals. If you are looking to invest outside the city, then it would be advisable to go for single-family homes. On the other hand, if you plan to invest in the city, townhouses would be the best option for you. Make sure that you analyze the properties thoroughly to warrant that you end up making the right investment decision.

Target Tenants

Property analysis also requires that you get to know the type of tenants that you will be dealing with. This is an important consideration as these are the people that would help you in setting off your loan. Thus, you need to know whether you will be renting out to reliable people or not. Considering the location that you will be investing in, you will be renting out for guys that switch jobs frequently. You might also rent out to individuals that are too picky with houses. So, knowing who your homes are meant for is crucial.

Occupancy and Vacancy Rates

Assuming that you will be purchasing a property that has been used before, you should take time to find out the occupancy and vacancy rates of the premises. How frequently do residents leave the place vacant? Also, what is the length of time that the rooms remain fully occupied? A good investment should be one that has a 100% occupancy rate. You get the most out of your investment. Well, there are times when your properties will be vacant, but this should not stay for long. The vacancy rate should tell you a lot, whether this is the place where you should invest your money or not.

Cash on Return

An experienced accountant in real estate business should help you evaluate the cash on a return that you anticipate getting on rental properties that you might invest in. Cash on return refers to the amount of money, in cash, that you gain after selling a property. Estimating this value prior to making your investment aids in making sound decisions on where you will earn increased returns on your investments.

Repairs

What is the condition of the property that you are about to purchase? If it is an old premise, you ought to mull over the type of repairs that are required to give a full facial uplift to the rentals. Are you comfortable with these repairs taking into consideration the budget that you have in mind? Maybe you are out looking for a property that simply needs painting or new roofing. Therefore, it is vital that you figure out whether the repairs are beyond your budget expectations. If this is the case, feel free to find an option that is within your budget range. Don't force yourself on residential houses that will demand more than you had budgeted for.

Chapter 14: How to Find the Best Rental Properties

A common question with regards to real estate investing is that of finding an ideal rental property. Both new and experienced investors would find it challenging to find the best rental properties. There are numerous things that need to be considered, which makes the process confusing. With the rise in the number of developers out there, one can never be sure of what to look for.

In some cases, you might require the help of an expert to ensure that you settle for a suitable property that will earn you profit. The importance of choosing an ideal rental property is the fact that it determines whether or not you will run a profitable business. If you end up choosing bad rentals, then you can be sure that you will make losses.

Conduct a Market Research

The first step that you should make is to conduct market research on the types of properties that exist. A thorough market analysis should reveal to you that particular properties perform well as compared to others. Also, you will have a deeper understanding of what renters often look for in rental properties. After evaluating the options that you have, you should make a decision on whether or not you will be investing in the market.

The Neighborhood

Assess the area where you wish to invest in and consider whether it is a comfortable place. Find out whether there are amenities that your residents will be enjoying in case you purchase the rental assets. These amenities typically motivate people to live in a particular surrounding. Therefore, it is essential that you confirm whether they exist or not.

Economic Situation

Your investment will only be profitable if you secured a place where a good number of people are working. Also, the population growth should tell you something about the viability of the property you are interested in. The best properties are located in areas where there is a high employment rate. This means that the cash flow in this area is high. Tenants in such an environment will not struggle to pay rent. Compare this to a place where a few people are employed. In this scenario, you will always fight with your renters since they delay paying their rent. So, it is vital that you evaluate the economic situation of the neighborhood that caught your attention.

Compare Many Deals

The best way of finding a good property that impresses you is by comparing many deals in the market. Limiting yourself to a few will only hinder you from spending what you think is the best form of investment. You might have come across the phrase that says you have to kiss several frogs before finding the right price. Well, this also applies to real estates. Have multiple deals to compare from. Compare the prices, the locations, amenities and other appealing features that will lure your tenants. After making your comparison, you should consult local realtors to find out whether they are thinking in the same direction. If you find that you have similar ideas, then it is quite likely that it is the best deal that you ought to go for. The main issue is that you should not forget to do your own research.

Seek Help from Experts

Sometimes getting the best rental deals in the market demands that you make good use of what's available in the market. Real estate agents could help in making the searching process relatively easy. You should rely on a local real estate agent. They have all the info you need to find a lucrative rental property in the neighborhood you are interested in.

Consider Unique Attributes

When choosing ideal rental properties, there are several things that you will be focusing on. Well, price is one of the main things you will have to focus on. You will also take your time to consider other additional features that make the premises worth investing. For instance, you will have to confirm the amount of taxes that you will be paying. Depending on the amount of taxes you will be incurring you can go ahead and make your mind whether this is the property for you. High taxes should not discourage you from investing in a property. If the location is promising, you can take the risk and invest here.

Finding the right neighborhoods

When it comes to deciding on where to look for your first rental property, the first thing you will need to consider is if you plan on being an active landlord or having someone else manage the day to day operations of your rental property for you.

On the contrary, if you plan on utilizing a property management company, then you will want to most likely focus on a multifamily property as many management services won't work with just a single residence or a single-family home.

Consider the location

This is more than merely scouting the rental prices of homes in a given area, and it requires a "feet-on-the-ground" or simply doing some footwork approach for the best results. Assuming you are looking for a rental property with a specific type of tenant in mind, then you will want to head out into various neighborhoods and get a feel for them and the types of people that call them home. You will also want to take into account the general upkeep and feeling of safety that naturally comes as part of the neighborhood as this will affect how much you can charge for the property as well as the types of tenants you will attract. When it comes to finding out the real scoop about an area, the best people you can hope to talk to are other individuals who are already renting in a particular area.

Always look for houses or real estate properties that have just come on the market.

There may be a lot more competition with these types of homes or real estate properties that have just come on the market. However, you will be able to get a real estate deal that is a better deal than a real estate property that has sat on the market for a long time.

If you are quick and offer the right amount money for the real estate property, you will probably get the real estate property before other investors even have a chance to check it out. The biggest problem with houses and other real estate properties that have been on the market for a long time is that there is a reason that they have been on the market for a long time.

Natural Disasters

If there are natural disasters in a particular area, you need to be aware of this. A location faced with natural disasters will require you to pay for insurance. This is an expense that will have an impact on your rental income. It is vital to know how much this will cost. Paying huge fees for insurance would only render your investment unprofitable. Think of finding the right place that is not linked to natural disasters.

Chapter 15: Managing Your Rentals

Property management sounds like an easy task, right? It might be an easy job for you, but you have to take your time in learning the essentials of managing your rentals successfully. The management process might differ, contingent on the type of properties that you will be managing. However, your primary focus should be to impress your renters. Winning over their love is the only way that they would stay longer on your premises without feeling the need to move out.

Renting Out Your Property

The last thing that you need in your rental properties is vacant rooms. This is not good for your real estate business. These rental rooms should not just be filled with people. They should be occupied by individuals that you can trust to pay their rent on time. Free yourself from the nightmare of allowing anyone to rent your properties. People are different. You need to have a plan of how you will evaluate your tenants before allowing them to reside in your investment.

Preparing Your Rentals

Prior to renting your houses, the first step is always to make sure that the rooms are livable. The rooms should be well set for tenants to move in and continue with their lives right away.

When preparing your rentals, you should think about your target market. Who are the people that you are targeting with your rentals? If you are targeting students, you should renovate the rooms to match student demands. If you are targeting individuals that have families, confirm that every room is designed is a way that entices a family setting. Have two separate bedrooms where one is the master bedroom, and the other is the bedroom for kids.

During the renovation process, you should not focus on the interior sections alone. The first impression is imperative. You need to give your rentals a facial uplift that will attract people walking down the street. Remember, the houses should appeal even to those that are not interested in renting. Through their word of mouth, they will inform their friends about the beautiful rentals that they could choose.

The renovation process will demand the help of an expert. This is something that you cannot do on your own. Talk to your real estate agent about your renovation plan. Chances are that if they have reliable contractors in town, they can link you up with them. A perfect finish is what you are after. This means that there is no room for mistakes.

After the renovation process is complete, you can't assume that the houses are ready to be rented. You should make a point of repeatedly inspecting for the best results. Ask yourself the questions that any tenant would want to know of. If there is something missing in the rentals, fix them accordingly.

Determining Your Rental Price

Knowing the right amount to charge your tenants as rent might be a challenging task. After completing your renovations, you will be worried about recovering the money that you used. As such, you will be tempted to raise the rent slightly higher to cater for the decorations that you made. Well, this is not the best move to take. This is because tenants will be careful to compare prices before renting your premises. Consequently, overpricing your houses will only have a negative impact on its demand.

The best way of estimating a reasonable rent to pay is by comparing prices with neighboring but similar rentals. This should give you a rough idea of what your target audience expects. To capture the market, you should set the price slightly higher or just below the market value. Renters will be impressed that your good looking houses are moderately priced.

Part of determining your rent requires that you estimate the amount of security deposit that you will demand from your tenants. You ought to know whether you will be setting limitations on refundable amounts on the security deposit. Different states have got different laws that touch on the security deposit. As a landlord, you should familiarize yourself with these laws and regulations.

Marketing Your Rentals

The next thing in line would be marketing your rentals. Without the right marketing, your rentals might stay longer without being occupied. This could be avoided if you chose to market your properties using the right marketing techniques.

Back in the day, marketing rentals would have taken time because homeowners would have to post ads on magazines. Today, things have changed. With the advent of the internet, everything is easy. You only need to spread the news on social media pages such as Facebook, Instagram, Twitter and several others. You will not be paying anything for this kind of marketing. The results will impress you since information spreads like wildfire on social media. You only need to remember to post several times. Also, encourage some of your friends to like and share your posts widely. You will be surprised at the overwhelming response that you will get.

Converting Interests into Visits

Successful marketing will be evident from the responses that you will be getting. It is important that you convert the responses into visits. Your marketing technique should be to convince your target market that they need to visit the houses in person. When showing your properties to interested parties, this is where you get to win them over. The right strategies will ensure that they do not leave without making up their minds.

Showing off your premises by simply stating the obvious things is not what you should be doing. Focus on the pros of your rental properties. Give your visitors a chance of comparing the good things that they will be getting if they chose to reside in your estates. The bonuses that you offer them will give them an assurance that your houses are worth going for.

Selecting Your Tenants

With everything ready around your houses, the last step would be to select your tenants. This sounds like an easy-to-do process. However, it should be noted that it takes time to get the right audience coming your way. Knowing who to pick will affect your investment. Undeniably, if you settle for the wrong tenants, you will regret investing in real estates.

Managing your properties is nothing close to a dating game. Regardless, you still need to take time to know who your tenants are. Gathering their personal information should be done in accordance with the housing laws that are stipulated in your area of residence. A natural process that renters have to go through is that they should fill out an application and deliver it to the landlord. The landlord then verifies their information and evaluates whether or not they are fit to live on the premises. After that, the landlord communicates their verdict to successful applicants. This is a similar process that you will have to put your tenants through.

Managing Tenant Movement

Another critical factor during the property management process is knowing how to deal with tenants as they move in and out of your property. Of course, the best time would be when the tenants will be moving in. This is the time where you need to capitalize on informing your renters about the rules and regulations of your premises. As the owner of the premises, you will want to inform your tenants more about the payment dates and deadlines for paying rent. Giving them a smooth experience from the word go guarantees that you welcome your renters in the right way.

Your worst moment would be when your tenant decides to shift to a new location. Perhaps they would be moving because they are changing jobs or that they are looking for a bigger house. The reasons don't matter. What matters most is how you manage this movement. It is imperative that you understand the laws regulating such movement. Your renter will request for their rent deposit. You need to figure out if you will be using part of the money to cater for renovation expenses.

Collecting Rent

The first time you interact with your tenant determines whether or not they will be paying their rent on time. This is something that you need to make clear with your renter the moment they make a decision of renting your premises. Ask them all the questions that you need regarding rent payment. If possible, you should also motivate them to ask you anything concerning rent. Dealing with them effectively will depend on whether they pay rent on time.

As a good property manager, you need to understand that the worst can happen to your renters and they might fail to pay their rents on time. You need to act like a human being and understand such circumstances. There are times when the tenants would fail to pay their rents even after the grace period has elapsed. Legally, you are allowed to take the necessary steps to regain control of your rental properties. No harm intended, but you are running a business. There are expenses to take care of not forgetting the fact that your mortgage loan needs to be paid. For that matter, your leniency should not exceed expectations as it could ruin your business in the long run.

Dealing with Troublesome Tenants

In the course your property management experience, there is no doubt that you will have to deal with tenants that drain energy from you. These are the individuals that have a habit of failing to pay their rent on time. Also, they will misuse your property by destroying it without considering the amount of money you invested in having such a beautiful home. The question is; how do you deal with them?

When dealing with tenants that do not pay their rent on time, it is best that you offer your renters a written document detailing to them about the policies that are in your premises. This should act as a reminder that it is important that they pay their rent on time.

You could also avoid the idea of dealing with loud tenants by making your rental policies clear. Communicate your rules and regulations effectively. This will give your renters a good reason to respect you by taking good care of your investment. You should note that one single renter can affect the entire business that you are running. Ensure that you effectively deal with problems the moment they arise.

Maintaining the Rental Properties

The best way of owning a rental property is by effectively maintaining it. The maintenance process is something that you can do on your own if at all, you have a few rental units. When you increase the size of your investment, you will need the help of professionals to warrant that the maintenance process is done smoothly. For larger premises, piling up the maintenance demands will only affect your good relationship with your tenants. In such instances, you need to hire an on-site manager to oversee the maintenance process on a regular basis. This will help in making sure that issues are attended to the moment they arise. Undeniably, this is the right way of keeping your renters happy.

Protecting Your Rental Properties

Successful management process also entails protecting your rental properties. Your property is an investment that you made with the hopes of earning profit out of it. It, therefore, makes a lot of sense if you take the necessary measures to safeguard it. Unexpected circumstances could occur, including bad weather. You should be aware of these risks and make sure that you cover your premises against such issues. Take time to choose insurance providers that will cover your home against several issues including weather, theft, fire and many more. You took a lot of time to invest in real estates, losing your property could happen in days. Make a wise move by covering it with the appropriate coverage.

Chapter 16: Top Features that Make a Profitable Real Estate Investment

Look out for the following elements while you search for a property to buy that will result in a profitable real estate investment.

Property Taxes

Property taxes are not uniform across the states, and even across different areas in the same state. You are an investor hoping to have a steady income from your property. For this, you must be aware of how much rent will go towards property taxes. It is also important to note that high taxes need not be a bad thing at all provided the neighborhood is excellent enough to retain tenants for a sustained period of time ensuring your cash flows are good, and your vacancy rates are low.

Crime Rates

If the crime rate in the neighborhood of your potential rental property is high, then it might be a wise thing to call off the deal. After all, no one wants to live in an area that is a hotspot for criminal activity. The public library and/or the police station in the locality are good places to check out accurate figures for crime rates.

You will have to check out the figures for different types of crimes, including serious crime, vandalism, petty crimes, and what is the latest activity in the area. Have the crime rates go up or down? While at this point, you can also check out the frequency of police patrol in the concerned locality.

Natural Disasters

Insurance for your property is a significant cost that will affect your cash flows and ROI. You should know the cost of all the insurances needed for your rental home before you invest in it. If the locality is prone to natural disasters such as forest fires, floods, earthquakes, etc., then your insurance could be so high that the rent is not sufficient to cover costs.

Job Market

Localities close to areas which have the potential for employment opportunities tend to attract tenants. For example, if you know that a major company is opening a branch office or even moving their central office to the said locality, you can rest assured your property will be an excellent investment for rental income as workers and employees of the said company are bound to move here.

Rents

After all, you are investing in property to earn rent, which is going to be a primary source of income for you. Therefore, one of the first elements you need to check out is the kind of rents you can expect for your property. Real estate agents will have details of the average rent in the concerned area.

If the average rent does not result in positive cash flow for you, then you have to continue your hunt for a good rental property. In addition to the present average cash flows, you must determine future cash flows too.

If there is a lot of development planned in the area, and the property taxes are going to be increased in the future, then it could be likely that you cannot afford to keep the property because cash flows are not lucrative enough for you. Therefore, find out about current average rents, and try to gauge the future trend.

Schools

If your rental property is for families, then you must consider the quality of local public schools and other educational facilities. If your property is excellent, but the schools are not reputed, then the appreciation value and the rental income from your property will be negatively impacted. So, check for schools and other learning places before deciding on buying the property.

Neighborhood

The quality of neighborhood that houses your rental property influences two important investment factors; the type of tenants and vacancy rates. Both these factors have a direct impact on your cash flows and ROI. Therefore, it is important to choose a neighborhood that is suitable for the types of tenants who can afford the rent you need to earn to make your real estate investment profitable.

For example, if you buy a rental property in a neighborhood that is close to a university, the chances of students being your tenants are high. If you take students as tenants, then you will encounter vacancies frequently, especially during university breaks. Again, there are no right or wrong choices. Be aware of such situations before choosing to invest in rental properties and ensure your investment strategy is in line with your goals.

Amenities

Scout the locality for current and future amenities for its residents. Look out for parks, malls, shopping areas, proximity to metro and bus stations, movie theaters, restaurants, and more. Most city municipalities issue pamphlets and brochures speaking of upcoming projects in various localities and neighborhoods.

Future Developments

Find out as much information as you can about the property and the locality. The best people you can get accurate information on rent are current tenants in that area. Renters tend to be more honest about the problems in the area because they have no investment there. Brokers and homeowners, on the other hand, could try to underplay issues prevalent in the area for vested interests.

When you finally identify an excellent rental property, remember to get your own finances in order, and keep realistic expectations from your investment. Your finances should be robust enough to give you time to wait for the property to begin generating positive cash flows. Don't invest in a rental property when you are in financial doldrums. The chances of making irreversible mistakes are high when you are desperate for your rental income to start generating cash before it is ready.

Chapter 17: What are the Risks Involved?

There are definitely advantages to investing in rental properties. You can earn a lot of passive income and make high profits, all while maintaining financial security for the future. And while owning rental properties can be relatively safe, there are risks involved. It's good to practice diligence and ensure that if any of the negatives happen, you'll know how to turn it around quickly, before losing any money.

Vacancy

Having a high amount of vacancies is probably one of the worst things to happen to a rental property owner. Tenants are how you make your money and income, so going without them means you go without money. Do the proper research about the different areas; figure out which neighborhoods are safest, and which ones yield the best amenities. It might end up being a little more expensive to buy a property in a better neighborhood, but tenants are more likely to rent where they feel safe and where they have a lot of different things to choose from. Keeping savings specifically for vacancies would probably be the smart thing to do, just in case you end up having to pay the mortgage, insurance, and property taxes from your own money.

Bad Tenants

While dealing with vacancies can mean you might lose money, having bad tenants can be so much worse. There's a huge risk when taking in unknown people, and it requires you to be pretty selective. You need to do background checks, get references from previous landlords, ask for proof of income, run a credit check, and make sure to take a security deposit. If you end up with the wrong tenant, it could cost you a lot more than having the room empty for a bit. Make sure you also listen to what your gut is telling you. A person could be great on paper; have the necessary paperwork, have excellent credit, and great references. But if there's just something odd about them, and they're giving you a strange vibe, then there might be something off about them that would mean they're not a good tenant. Trust yourself!

Cash Flow

Triple check the expenses and how much everything will cost you; even put in the cost of random maintenance that might actually never happen. Underestimating the cost could mean the end of your business, and you are owing thousands. Having the right team to help can make sure you don't accidentally forget something, but ultimately, it's up to you to remember. And it's not just considering the upfront costs, but how much everything will cost you each month. If you end up losing money every month because of not realizing the cost, you'll eventually be out of business from paying out of pocket.

The Right Time to Buy

Just like in other markets, the real estate market also has a sort of supply and demand. There's a constant fluctuate, so if you're thinking of maybe selling your property down the road, you might end up not making a profit. Investing in rental properties can cost a lot of money, especially up front, so you want to make sure that your expected return in the future makes actually worth making the investment in the first place. The best thing to do is see if it's a seller's or buyer's market, and keep up with the trends. You want to buy in a buyer's market and sell once it's circled back around to a seller's market.

Theft

There's always a risk of your property becoming burglarized, especially if you're in a lower income location. If the crime rate is on the higher side, then you'll end up with a high turnover of tenants. Plus, what you charge for rent will be much lower than what you could charge in a higher income location. If burglary does happen a lot in your location, you could end up paying a lot of money in legal procedures and fees.

Foreclosure

If you end up not making enough profit, and can't meet your mortgage payments, then there's the change of your property being foreclosed. That's definitely the last thing you want because not only can it hurt you being approved for any future real estate loans, but the word might get around, and no one would want to rent from you. Knowing the numbers and making sure you'll get a profit can help minimize the chance, plus making sure you have emergency savings to help you out if needed.

Maintenance

Especially at the beginning, before you hire someone, you'll probably be the person your tenants call when something goes wrong. There's a high level of work involved when running rental properties, and that included maintenance issues. What happens when a pipe bursts? You can't just let it sit and hope it fixes itself. And if it happens in the middle of the night, there's a high chance that you won't be able to get anyone out to fix it until the next morning. Knowing basic maintenance can be very helpful as a landlord, and help you to save spending more money on issues that end up becoming a lot worse. Or if you're not very handy, you can hire a property manager that does know how to fix those types of thing. Keep in mind too that eventually, properties start to show their age. They typically start having structural damage, and major things would need replacing. It's best to keep up with everything, because if you let it go, then it'll just get worse and cost you a lot more money than necessary.

Chapter 18: How to Know When to Exit

There might come a time when you're ready to sell your rental property. It makes sense to keep it long term, and there are many benefits to actually never selling. But maybe you're tired of dealing with tenants and repair issues, maybe it's a good time to sell, and you'd like to make a nice profit. Or maybe you just want to get out of the game. Regardless of your reasoning, there are some very specific factors to take into consideration when you realize it's time to sell your rental property:

Life

 It happens, we get it. You can have a major life event, something that makes you reconsider owning your properties. Maybe a family member died, maybe you were laid off and no longer had the right funds to help support yourself, maybe you have to move across the country. You end up spending a lot of time and money focusing on whatever event is happening, so much so that you just don't have time to deal with your properties. It's possible that you can sell all of them, or maybe just downsize to one or two, enough for a little passive income.

More Money

It's entirely possible that you end up making a lot more money elsewhere. You could have another revenue source that really took off, or maybe you have a full-time job that just offered a great promotion. Rental income is considered passive income, but it also takes a lot of effort. If you can get more money from somewhere else that takes less effort, then it makes a lot more sense to go with that other option.

Not Enough Money

While you'd love if everyone loves your property, you have terrific tenants and are making a significant income each month, there's a chance that you could end up with negative cash flow instead. When investing in rentals, it's important to be making an income off of them in the first month. If you've gone months without any profits, and in fact are in the negatives, then maybe it's time to reevaluate this property and whether it's worth it.

Unhappy

Maybe you're just unhappy with how things are in your life now. You were excited about investing in rental properties at first, but now it's just too much work with no reward. Why would you keep doing something that makes you unhappy? Being a landlord can be a stressful job. That stress might be something you overlook because you're making great money and getting incredible profits. But eventually, it can become a burden and weigh pretty heavy on you. You end up with a ton of anxiety and stress that never really goes away. And not only is that a lot to deal with, but it's also awful for your health! You don't want a heart attack just because you're unhappy in your job, do you?

Too Much

Real estate is all about supply and demand. If there are too many houses on the market, then the selling price will go down. That's definitely something you'd like to avoid, but it might be inevitable. While houses are sold and bought all the time, if there are new homes being built, then it will be a very long time before it's a seller's market. Housing for sale or rent will become oversaturated and flooded. If you notice that there are a ton of new houses or condos being built, it's best to sell before they're finished, or you'll end up having to wait until it comes back around. Which could take decades, so you need to figure out if you want to keep renting that long or not.

Taxes

Property taxes are a pain. They can cause a lot of hassle and upset feelings, and they're something the local and state governments keep increasing instead of going somewhere else. Basically, if the local government has a big project in the works, like filling in all the potholes, they just decide to raise property taxes instead of increasing road tolls. This means that with higher property taxes, then the rent increases as well. The issue with this, though is that increasing rent takes some time. It might say on your lease that you can't raise the rent until the lease is over.

Major Repairs

There are typically significant expenses that happen like clockwork - a roof needs to be replaced every 10 to 20 years, a new water heater every 10 to 15 years, etc. These are normal, and you'll figure them into your housing costs at the beginning of the buying process. However, it's possible your property ends up needing repairs that cost more than it's worth. A law was recently passed in San Francisco that meant any housing units over a garage had to be retrofitted, which costs anywhere from $100,000 to $300,000. That's a lot of money to spend all at once, or even in a payment plan. You need to assess your property and decide if it's worth fixing or worth more just to sell it.

Commission Rates

The commission rate for real estate agents has been steady at a very high 5 percent, which isn't much of a difference from the 6 percent that was ten years ago! The main issue is that half of the 5 percent, 2.5 percent, goes to the buyer's real estate agent. They obviously want the best possible deal for their client, which means the best possible deal for them. You're basically paying the buyer's real estate agent instead of their own client. And most real estate agents try to find listings that have the 2.5

percent commission, so if yours doesn't, then it will be doubly challenging to sell. If by some chance the commission rate goes down, then take the chance before it changes again by selling.

Appreciate the Property

There is such a thing as the property having "appreciation." This is when the value of the property goes up, and it becomes worth it to sell. Let's say you decide to invest in a fixer-upper for your rental property. You completely overhaul it; new furniture, new appliances, new everything. Your plan is to rent it out, and you're successfully making a great profit from it. However, there's a chance that because the property is so high now, and if the location becomes more up and coming and hip, then the value of the property goes way up. When that happens, you need to decide whether you'd like to keep renting it out or sell it. If you do sell, you could use some of that money to put back into a different property instead.

Chapter 19: How Does Real Estate Investing Make Money?

The real estate investor makes money in many ways, but there are four definitive places where the investor will profit. First, real estate is often viewed as a safe or smart investment because real estate appreciates rather than depreciates over time. Unlike a car, which loses several hundred dollars' worths of value the minute you drive it off the dealership's lot, a piece of property – with or without a building on site – tends to grow in value rather than lose it. Many issues can affect the appreciation of your property. If you purchase a home that you intend to make a rental, then the homes around it can help to add value to your rental property. If your rental property is a commercial lot, then any new businesses opened nearby will help to increase your property. Those upgrades mentioned earlier that can help you to save at tax time? Those can add value to your property as well. Very rarely does a piece of property lose value, and, when it does, it is generally due to changes in the overall real estate market.

Next, as an investor, you can plan to create related income as well as cash flow income. Real estate related income can include the money made a sell by selling a piece of property, but often, many investors see this income when they purchase a piece of property and "flip" it. You may have seen reality television shows about small businesses who purchase foreclosed homes, make improvements to the home, then "flip" it, or sell it for a profit (which includes recouping one's capital tied into making said improvements). Of course, as one interested in creating a passive income, this might not be for you, but, we will discuss the possibilities and the profitability of such a business venture.

You'll want to calculate and evaluate the risk versus the reward of investing in real estate property. The primary reward of purchasing real estate as an investment is the passive income that you'll receive from owning a piece of real estate. You might not initially make enough money to quit your day job, but you can still generate income with little effort on your part other than general maintenance on your property. Speaking of income, if you crunch the numbers with your financial advisor, pick up a property that is reasonably priced, and charge a reasonable amount of rent that will cover your costs, you'll create another source of income from owning rental property. Furthermore, rental property generally appreciates in value; this means that you'll see your personal asset value grow as a result of owning this property. Speaking of assets, you will find that you are entitled to many significant tax deductions as a result of owning real estate property. Finally, the real estate market is often more stable than the stock market, so investing in real estate is often a safer bet than stocks as far as investing in your money goes.

When it comes to the risks of investing in real estate property, there are a few. It is prudent to weigh the risks and determine if they are risks you can live with should you decide upon this type of investment. The highest risk in real estate property is often the very entity which helps you as the landlord to create income – the tenant(s). Tenants can be pleasant, or they can be a nightmare. Unfortunately, you can utilize all the background checks available and still end up with a "dud" for a tenant. Some tenants complain regularly and expect you, the landlord, to tend to their concerns. This is why it is so important to not only document in pictures the condition of the property prior to renting the unit, but also to have an outside official come in to inspect the home and ensure that everything works as it should. You can hire a home inspector to come in and check the lighting and plumbing as well as appliances prior to the new tenant's occupation of the rental property. Another good rule of thumb is to do a move-in inspection with the tenant, with each of you signing off that there are no issues (or documenting an issue that you must correct) prior to the beginning of the lease. Any time you can document inspections, payments, background checks, or anything that might be questioned later, you are saving yourself legal trouble later on. Next, you may have tax breaks because you own a rental property, but if you meet certain income levels, you may have to pay in the form of a surtax rather than benefit from tax deductions due to your real estate property. Keep in mind that although passive income from real estate is typically a benefit to you, you may experience a time when the housing market is once again not doing well, or you may simply have decided real estate is not the investment for you. If this becomes the case, you may spend a good bit of money to get out of your real estate property. Furthermore, you can't sell a portion of rental income (not typically; you can't sell half the house, but you can sell a portion of land you purchased while still retaining a single-family unit home. Finally, you can count on being responsible for paying all the costs of the property should you find yourself without a tenant.

Chapter 20: How to Handle Failure in the Real Estate Market

When it comes to getting started with the rental property market, it may seem a bit overwhelming. You want to be able to bring in the nice steady income that comes from this kind of investment, but there is a lot of risks, and you may be worried about whether it is the right choice for you to work with or not.

Even when you follow some of the rules and tips that we suggest in this guidebook, there are times when you may fail in real estate. It is a hard game to play, and being able to figure out what is best for your customers and what road you should take sometimes is hard. You may go and do some research, and then find that your "perfect" rental property is not one that tenants want. You may spend hours researching and never find the property that feels like the right one to you. You may get some bad tenants who destroy the property, and you aren't sure if you are able to fix the damage and get the business back up and running.

There are times when you will do all of the work that you can and feel like you failed. But the difference between the successful rental property investors and those who will tell you it is a scam is that the successful ones didn't just give up and call it quits after one stumble.

If you are the kind of person who runs into trouble and then decides to run away, then these rental properties are not going to be the right option for you. It may sound mean, but if you want things to be easy, go and use a savings account rather than rental properties. This market is tight, and you are going to fair at some point or another.

The neat thing though is that you do have the option to get through it. You don't have to meet the failure and think that it is time to give up. Instead, you can take a look at that failure and decide that it is a learning experience. You can then take that learning experience and turn it around to ensure that you will see better results next time.

Maybe it will cost more to fix up the property, but does that still fit into your budget? Maybe you will take in a bit less profit overall, but will this help you to make more money overall because you made the place look beautiful. If you are still able to do the rental property with the fixes and make a good income, then that is definitely an option to go with.

Or, maybe the costs will be a bit too much to make an excellent rental profit still each month. But you notice that there seems to be an uptrend to the market that is coming up, and you estimate that in the next six months or so, the housing market will be going crazy. Maybe you decide to invest in fixing up the property and then sell it in a flip and make some money there. Yes, you want to concentrate on doing rentals, but this method at least lets you recover your money, plus maybe a bit more, and then you can move on to looking for the next rental property.

If the work is just too much to work with and you can't afford it, maybe it is time to look at selling it to another investor. Even making a few thousand on it can be a good idea, and another investor can benefit from what you don't want to work with.

As you can see, there are options available to you. As a beginner, you may find out that you messed up by not doing the inspections and will assume that all is lost. You may assume that you won't be able to make any profits on the property and give up. But just from the above, there are three other options that you can choose to go with to reclaim at least a little bit of your profit and still stay in the game.

Another issue that you may face is that of tenants. One of these is the lack of being able to find good tenants, and another one is that you find tenants, but they end up being bad for the property and destroy it every chance that they get. Each of these can be bad. The first one means that you aren't getting any rental income. The second one means that you are going to probably not make any income, and even if you do, the costs of fixing up the mess can be really high.

When it comes to not being able to find any of the tenants you would like to work with, you may need to take a step back and consider why tenants aren't interested in the property. You should have done this research before, but as a beginner, there may have been things you missed out on. Instead of looking at this vacancy as something that will end your investment, it is time to get creative and figure out what you can do.

Maybe you need to go through and fix up some more of the things in the property. First, start out by having some people you know, maybe even some other rental property investors if you can, go through the property with you. They can point out some of the things that your tenants may want to be fixed, and you can work on improving those to get more people in the door.

Another option is to add in some other incentive. Maybe the rent is too high. You can consider dropping it down a little bit to see if that will bring in more tenants to at least look at the property. Or, you can choose to add a lowered deposit, the first month of rent free, or some other help or assistance to the tenant to entice them to pick your property.

When it comes to bad tenants, you need to be careful with your screening process. You want to make sure that you are picking out good tenants. You want them to have a steady job history so that it is more likely they will pay you on time each month. You want them to have a good credit score, good references, and to be reliable so that they will take care of the property that you are renting out to them.

A bad tenant can quickly get into your property if you don't go through and do the right evaluations and reviews on them before you let them move into the property. This can take a lot of work and will cost a bit of money when you are getting started, but it is definitely something that is worth your time to consider doing.

If a lousy tenant gets in there, it is important to be careful. Yes, you want to get them out of there as soon as possible so that you can start to regain some of your loss and start earning some profits again. But you also don't want to go against some of the laws in your area. There are laws out there that protect the tenants, and these are often going to be more geared towards the tenant than towards you. Just because you want them to get out of there, don't make the issue worse or cause a bigger failure because you started doing things that are considered against the law.

For beginners, if you are dealing with a bad tenant, consider finding some legal help. This can at least provide you with some advice on what you can legally do to either get your money back if the tenants left town without paying and with a messy property behind them, or even if you need to start looking at evicting the tenants because they won't pay. They can walk you through the legal steps so that you can take care of these tenants and get them out of your property once and for all.

But just because you ended up with one lousy tenant doesn't mean that all of your investments are over. Yes, this is a setback, and you probably did lose some money. If the tenants weren't paying their rent during this time, you were the one who had to deal with the mortgage for those months. If they left a mess behind in the property, then you are the one who has to clean it up and get everything fixed. But you can definitely use this as a kind of learning experience.

One bad tenant is something that you will find in common with all of the successful rental property investors that you come across. They have all, at one point or another, dealt with a tenant who didn't pay the bills, who didn't take care of the property or caused issues in some other way. But they didn't give up after one bad tenant. And if you want to make this one property into a rental empire, then you must make sure that you are willing to learn some lessons from that bad tenant, and then keep moving forward to do better next time.

Another issue that we will discuss here is the idea of real estate market failure. Sometimes this is going to catch you by surprise because you were not certain about how the market cycle works and missed out on the signs. Other times the market failure is a complete surprise and you, along with many other investors, were caught off guard by this.

When you look at the market for real estate, you will notice that it has been doing well with growth over the past few years. This is an excellent thing for those who want to invest in real estate, but there is never a guarantee that this trend is going to continue in the future. One of the risks that you are going to face when you work on this market is the concentration of assets. For most investors, owning even one property for renting out is a large concentration of assets because they will need to use a major amount of their net worth, and it all goes to the same investment.

As a landlord, at least until you can really build up the empire and make it strong, your investment is not going to be that diversified. If the national economy or even your local economy starts to go downhill, even a little bit, this means that you risk losing a lot of money, thanks to depreciation.

One of the options that you do have available to help you out with this risk is to diversify the investment as much as you can. For this to work, you may decide to find a few other investors and launch your own residential investment company. This is basically going to be a small business that will buy, sell, and rent out properties.

The point of this is going to be pretty similar to what you would do on your own as an individual investor, but it gives you the possibility of distributing your money as shares in several properties in different cities, states, and so on, without having to come up with all of the cash on your own.

Conclusion

Thank you for making it to the end of this book, figure out where you go from here. It might be best to start slow, maybe even speak to several real estate investors for their opinions and how they got started. Or you could just jump right in and start researching properties and their locations. Remember, location is everything to your success, so it's best to look up several properties and then look around at the different amenities they have. You could even do it opposite; if there's an area that you really like and know will do really well, look up if there are any properties for sale in it. Look at apartments, single family homes, and multi-family homes to see which ones you'd prefer and which ones would do the best in the area you're interested in. And don't forget, you can look at the properties first, but make sure your right next step is figuring out exactly how much you can afford. But this book can really help you figure things out without getting overwhelmed and truly help you to succeed.

Doing the research, setting up budget goals, and learning about the areas where you would like to invest are keys to achieving success.

The next step in your real estate endeavors is to put the information you found in this book to practice. Investing in profitable real estate rental properties can, at first, seem daunting. But with the information provided in this e-book, you should be able to begin investing in real estate rental properties better equipped than when you first began to read it.

Do whatever it takes to get you into the frame of mind that allows you to see the business you are in clearly, and see what you have to do in a way that advances your goals rather than diminishes them. Real estate investing can be the doorway to financial security, financial freedom and even wealth-building, but it all starts with how much of your mind you want to invest.

Real estate investing is a path that opens up many other opportunities. If you are lagging out of fear, it will be at the cost of success. Do you want to give up on progress and a good income? You wouldn't want it! Hence, you must garner all the possible information from this guide and utilize it in your investing journey.

www.ingramcontent.com/pod-product-compliance
Lightning Source LLC
Chambersburg PA
CBHW021829170526
45157CB00007B/2725